NEW TECHNOLOGY

sports technology

Stewart Ross

Evans

Published by Evans Brothers Limited

Evans Brothers Limited
2A Portman Mansions
Chiltern Street
London W1U 6NR

First published 2011

British Library Cataloguing in
Publication Data
Ross, Stewart.
    Sports technology. -- (New technology)
    1. Sports--Technological innovations--
    Juvenile literature.
    I. Title II. Series
    796-dc22

    ISBN-13: 9780237540777

Printed by New Era Printing Co. Ltd China

Credits
Series editor: Paul Humphrey
Editors: Kathryn Walker and Helen Dwyer
Designer: sprout.uk.com
Production: Jenny Mulvanny
Picture researchers: Kathryn Walker
    & Rachel Tisdale

Acknowledgements
Cover and title page Guang Niu/Getty
Images; p.6 Kerim Okten/epa/Corbis;
p.7 Fernando Medina/NBAE/Getty Images;
p.8 photogolfer/Shutterstock; p.10 Adidas;
p.11 International Tennis Federation; p.12
HEAD UK; p.13 Bill Florence/Shutterstock;
p.14 Caryn Levy/PGA Tour/Getty Images;
p.15 Herbert Kratky/Shutterstock; p.16
Reuters/Seiko/Corbis; p.17 Fabrice
Coffrini/AFP/Getty Images; p.18 Cameron
Spencer/Getty Images; p.19 Al Messerschmidt/
Getty Images; p.20 Bjorn Larsson Rosvall/
AFP/Getty Images; p. 21 Hawk-Eye
Innovations; p.23 Michael Steele/Getty
Images; p.25 Scott Cunningham/Getty
Images; p.27 Eye of Science/Science
Photo Library; p.29 Adidas; p.30 Marek
Slusarczyk/Shutterstock; p.31 Andrzej
Burak/Shutterstock; p.32 Karim Sahib/
AFP/Getty Images; p.34 Janek Skarzynski/
AFP/Getty Images; p.35 Liu Jin/AFP/Getty
Images; p.36 Philippe Psaila/Science Photo
Library; p.37 Sean Aidan/Eye Ubiquitous/
Corbis; p.38 Odd Andersen/AFP/Getty
Images; p.39 Jeff Vinnick/Getty Images;
p.40 John Zich/AFP/Getty Images;
p.41 Drazen Vukelic/Shutterstock;
p.42 Sportphotographer.eu/Shutterstock;
p.43 bluecrayola/Shutterstock.

contents

introduction

During the 2009 World Swimming Championships, world records were broken every day. They tumbled so fast that even the journalists covering the event were not able to keep track. The reason? The sudden speeding up did not come from training or technique but from technology: nearly all the record-breakers were wearing a new type of 100 per cent polyurethane swimsuit.

Two revolutions There have been two revolutions in world sport. The first began a little over a century ago and saw the emergence of professionalism supported by vast crowds packed into huge stadiums. The second revolution

Technology too far? Polyurethane swimsuits in action at the 2009 World Championships, where dozens of records were broken. The suits were later banned because they enhanced the wearer's performance artificially.

is going on now. It is happening because technology is being applied to just about every aspect of sport, from the composition of tennis rackets to electronic decision-making and performance-improving drugs and therapies.

Some welcome the change, others hate it. Before we hasten to judge, it is worth remembering the enormous benefits that technology brings.

HOW IT WORKS

Swimsuits made of polyurethane, a form of plastic, contain no textiles. They fit over the body so tightly that they can take half an hour to get on. Once in place, they compress the muscles. This does away with unwanted muscle movement that can slow a swimmer down. Some critics say the suits also trap air inside, giving the swimmer greater buoyancy.

Referees turn to the video replay screen to check the crucial final shot of a basketball game in which the Houston Rockets overcame the Orlando Magic, 96-94.

These include a range of new sports, such as skateboarding and hang gliding, greater enjoyment through TV replays, more accurate decisions using video technology, and sporting opportunities for disabled athletes.

Success to the wealthy Set against these plusses are the negatives of technology. The most obvious is doping – taking substances that improve performance illegally. But there is also the cost of high-tech apparatus such as computerised training programmes and machines that measure how efficiently an athlete's body uses oxygen. Such things are so expensive that top-level success is often reserved for wealthy schools, colleges, clubs and countries.

FOR AND AGAINST

The pros and cons of electronic decision-making using video technologies.

For
- Electronic decision-making is more accurate than human referees or umpires.
- Decisions made by machines can be re-run for confirmation.
- Machines are more consistent than people: they do not have 'good' and 'bad' days.
- Machines cannot be biased in favour of one nation or player.

Against
- Some feel that judgement by technology reduces sport to the level of a computer game.
- Technology cannot yet take into account changing circumstances, such as the altered behaviour of a pitch after rain.
- Referring a decision to technology slows a game down.
- Where technology is used for some decisions but not others, the authority of the human judge is undermined.
- Technology cannot be used in value judgements, such as bad language or unsportsmanlike conduct.

CHAPTER 1
bats and balls

The most obvious impact of sporting technology is on the equipment we use. This generally means bats, clubs, sticks or rackets and the balls they strike. In most sports the effect of high-tech equipment is dramatic. Deep-grooved golf clubs, swinging footballs, carbon-fibre tennis rackets and springy hockey sticks all make modern sport, especially at the top level, faster and more power-based than ever.

Golf balls The way a golf ball moves through the air is affected by its composition, weight, size, shape and surface. To control the impact of technology, therefore, its design is tightly regulated. Engineers could, for instance, design a ball that flies huge distances. To prevent this, the sport's ruling bodies have said how far a golf ball can travel when hit with a specific force. This is the Overall Distance Standard (ODS), which

Today's golf stars use the type of lightweight carbon-fibre driver whose power and accuracy threatens to make most traditional golf courses too easy.

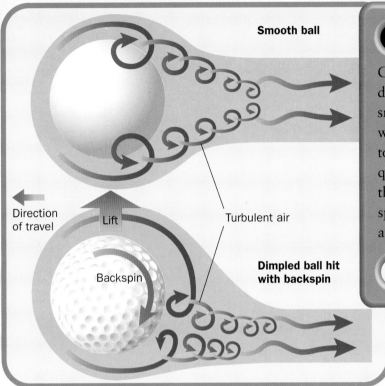

Smooth ball

Direction of travel

Lift

Backspin

Turbulent air

Dimpled ball hit with backspin

HOW IT WORKS

Contrary to what one might expect, a dimpled golf ball flies further than a smooth one. This is because when hit with backspin (spinning backwards towards the striker), the air moves more quickly over the upper surface than the lower one. The ball rises to fill the space above it created by the lack of air, and so travels faster and further.

The dimples on a golf ball scoop up the air and move it to the rear of the ball, where the air pressure remains high so there is less drag holding back the ball.

applies to all balls. It now stands at 290 metres (320 yards).

The way a golf ball spins affects how it performs. To gain distance, a golf ball needs to spin back towards the direction it has come from. However, this 'backspin' makes it stop more quickly when it lands, which is unhelpful for a long shot ('drive') intended to roll as far as possible. Nevertheless, backspin is essential when trying to stop the ball when it lands near the hole. Remarkably, designers have developed a ball that backspins slowly when hit for distance, but rapidly when the player wants it to stop dead on landing.

WHAT'S NEXT?

Scientists are working on golf balls with microchips inside. Using a phone with a satellite link, players would then be able to find a lost ball. The same technology could be used to line up a short range shot (putt), showing the player the right line for hitting the ball towards the hole when the ground is uneven. This technology, if permitted by the rules, would help a player line up a shot, but they would still have to hit it straight and at the right pace.

Footballs and tennis balls The modern football ball has fourteen panels compared with the old-style 32, and its surface of synthetic materials is virtually waterproof. The outer coating maximises the friction between boot and ball. This gives a kicker's boot greater grip on the ball, allowing them to spin it like a top. The result is a guided missile that is both light and capable of extraordinary flight paths. At the top level, any free kick awarded within 30 metres of the keeper is now a potential goal.

Basic tennis ball technology – a rubber sphere with a felt cover – is tightly regulated. The tennis balls used for official tournaments have to undergo a series of five tests to make sure they meet approved standards. Because racket power and playing surfaces have changed so much, the modern game uses four types of ball. According to the conditions, these tennis balls vary in size, bounce and the way they change shape under the pressure of a shot. As a consequence, technology and today's tennis are inseparable.

The match ball for the 2010 Football World Cup. For the first time, the outer panels have been moulded as parts of a sphere so the ball is perfectly round.

BRAIN SAVERS

In the old days, a leather football could double its weight as it absorbed water during a match played in wet weather. This meant heading the ball could give a player brain damage. Modern footballs are made of synthetic material or waterproofed leather and gain almost no weight in the wet. This helps to make the game quicker and more skilful – and saves the players' brains!

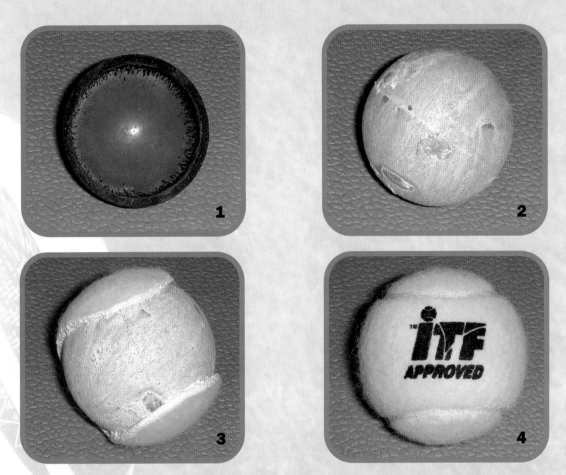

How a tennis ball is made. 1) A tennis ball starts as a moulded rubber half sphere. 2) Two of these half spheres are joined together. After compressed air is injected into the centre of the ball the two halves are sealed together to make a sphere and coated in a rubber solution. 3) A covering of mainly cotton, backed with a rubber solution, is placed over the ball. The ball is heated so that the rubber on the ball and the cloth sticks together. 4) The finished ball after it has been checked for quality.

Sophisticated sticks Today's field and ice hockey sticks offer power and precision to a degree that was unimaginable even 20 years ago. Much of this is due to the replacement of traditional wooden manufacture with a wide range of synthetic materials, including fibreglass, aramids and carbon fibre. The new sticks produce games that are both faster and harder. In addition, roller skate technology has generated an entirely new form of the game: roller hockey.

What a racket The latest tennis racket frames are put together using secret formulas from substances such as ceramics, aramids, boron and graphite. Today's frames are 300 per cent stiffer than older rackets. Because a stiff racket distorts less when striking the ball, the player has more control over where the ball goes. The racket head is also 40 per cent larger and the whole piece of apparatus is 30 per cent lighter than previous versions.

HOW IT WORKS

Some substances, including bone, certain crystals and a number of synthetic ceramics, are piezoelectric. This means (a) they generate electricity when under stress and (b) they become more rigid when a current is passed through them. The piezoelectric current created in a tennis racket by the stress of hitting the ball is amplified in the handle and fed back to the frame to stiffen it.

Racket strings are changing, too. Some players say the old strings made of cow gut cannot be improved on. Others have moved over to synthetic equivalents. Even more interesting are the latest anti-vibration measures using piezoelectric crystals. The electric current these crystals generate when the ball is struck is fed back into the ceramics of the frame. This causes it to stiffen, so cutting by up to 50 per cent the annoying vibration that may lead to injuries such as tennis elbow.

Beefy bats The size, shape and composition of cricket and baseball bats are strictly defined. The hefty modern cricket bat has scooped, or hollowed out, areas on the back of its blade to get the best power-for-weight ratio. Technology has certainly

This series of pictures shows what happens after a ball hits a tennis racket with piezoelectric crystals. The stress of the impact generates an electric current that stiffens the frame.

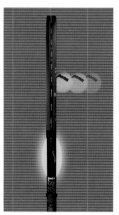 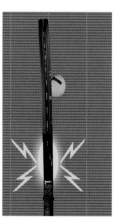 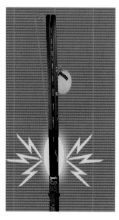 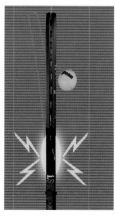 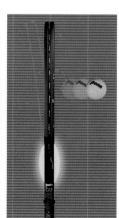

had a hand in producing the latest versions, including a doubled-bladed bat. This allows the ball to be hit with both the back and front of the bat, a great help in the short form of the game in which batters need to score runs as quickly as possible.

Professional baseball uses only traditional all-wood bats of maple or white ash. In the amateur game, however, bats are made from all kinds of other things, such as bamboo, aluminium, alloy and a range of modern hi-tech materials such as carbon fibre and aramids.

FOR AND AGAINST

Could new technology make baseball a better game?

For

- Radicals say baseball would be a more spectacular sport if players were allowed to use longer-hitting hi-tech composite bats.
- A pitcher could serve up more unplayable curveballs with a shinier baseball.
- These technological innovations would make baseball more exciting.

Against

- Baseball is about a player's skill, not how good their equipment is.
- Once new technology is allowed, one cannot predict how the game will change.
- Different bats and balls would make redundant all existing statistical records.

Of all the major sports, baseball has probably resisted most fiercely the impact of technology on its equipment.

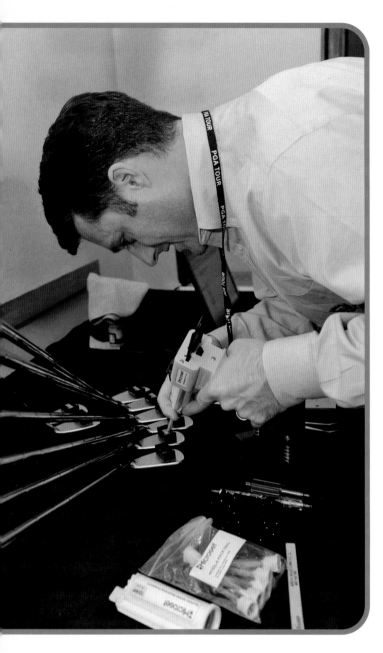

A scientific researcher checks the grooves on golf clubs to make sure that they conform to the official standard. Tiny variations in the grooves' size, shape and spacing can make all the difference to a tricky shot.

'Trampoline' golf clubs In the professional game, the shafts of golf clubs are made from carbon fibre reinforced polymer, giving the best strength-weight ratio. The heads are of three kinds: drivers for sending the ball a long way, irons for lofting the ball so it drops close to the hole, and putters for rolling it into the hole.

Technology could easily produce a driver capable of sending the ball over 450 metres (500 yards). This would make every golf course in the world redundant because players could hit the ball to the green with one shot rather than the two or three needed today for most holes. Modern drivers are hollow, with a face that acts like a springy trampoline when striking the ball. The spring of a club head is measured as its CoR (Coefficient of Restitution). To prevent golfing stars sending the ball right up to the hole with every drive, a club head's CoR may not be more than a stipulated figure (currently 0.83 CoR).

Irons have grooves along the club face to add the grip needed to get the ball spinning. By 2009, scientists had worked out the optimum spacing and shape of grooves to give players the greatest advantage when striking the ball in difficult situations, such as from long grass. This changed the art of golf so much so that steps were taken to ban clubs with U-shaped grooves, known as U-profile grooves.

Track and field equipment There are two areas in which technology has revolutionised track and field athletics: the javelin and the pole vault. The modern hollow javelin could be thrown beyond the central grassed area if technologists had not made it more difficult to 'fly'. They did this by moving its centre of gravity (the point of balance) away from the middle of the shaft. This made the javelin less aerodynamic, meaning its weight distribution and shape reduced the time it was in the air.

By allowing the pole to be made of any substance, the pole vault regulations are an open invitation to engineers to come up with something special. And they have. Today's pole is

The remarkable heights scaled by modern pole vaulters would be impossible without flexible fibreglass poles and artificial run up surfaces.

a specially shaped and super-bendy spring of fibreglass or similar material. The result? Records that stood at around 3.25 metres (men, 1900) and just over 4 metres (women, 1992) have today soared to 6 metres plus for men and 5 metres plus for women.

HOW IT WORKS

Air flowing over a javelin gives it a slight lift. This is greatest at the 'centre of pressure' – the place where the upward pressure is strongest. Because the centre of gravity is now in front of the centre of pressure, gravity pulls the nose of the javelin down. This reduces the length of a throw and makes more likely a nose-first landing, which is easier to mark.

CHAPTER 2
judgement

In 2004, a South African football referee shot dead a coach who had queried his decision. Extreme behaviour, maybe, but not that surprising: in major sports passions run very high indeed and officials are under extreme pressure. Many engineers believe that technology could make the situation easier because most sporting judgements are better made by machine than by fallible humans. Some say we should go even further and make the human referee redundant.

First past the post A modern photo-finish uses a high-speed digital camera taking 2,000 images a second. An object as small as a human hair can be detected. Even if a human eye could get near such precision, the brain behind it has no playback or freeze-frame facility for double checking. Cameras win every time.

False starts Technology improves athletics starts, too. The starting blocks from which sprinters push off are wired to the starting gun. If the block senses

Photo records of the finishing line, like this one showing Usain Bolt breaking the world 100 metre record in 2009, serve two functions. They separate the athletes as they cross the line and provide precise split-second timing.

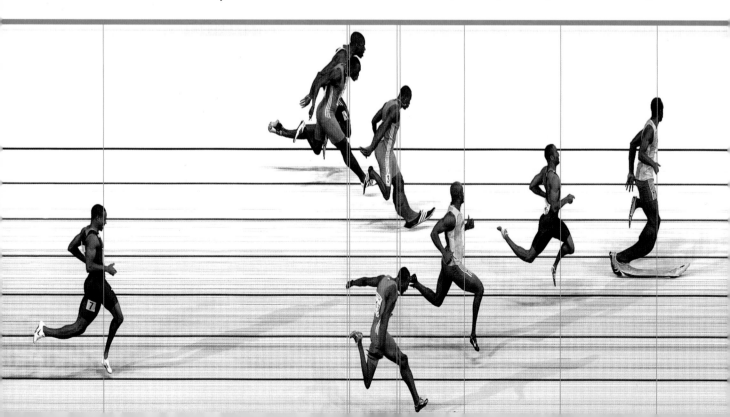

HOW IT WORKS

At sea level and in dry air at 20 °C (68 °F) sound travels at 1,236 kilometres per hour (768 mph). A sprinter on the outside of an athletics track, therefore, hears the starter's gun a fraction of a second later than a competitor in an inside lane. To ensure that all runners hear the gun at precisely the same time, each starting block is fitted with a speaker that relays the starter's commands.

A modern starting gun is wired to timing devices and to speakers behind the starting blocks in each lane.

pressure in less than 0.11 seconds (the fastest a human being can react) after the gun sounds, this means the athlete has started early. When this happens, a false start is recorded electronically against the offending lane.

Technology scores when it comes to distance measurement, too. A reflector placed in the ground where a shot, discus or javelin lands bounces back a laser beam – and the throw's precise length is flashed up in a split second.

Bang on time A stopwatch might be alright for timing your personal training but it's not much use when it comes to world records. Clock technology is also hard pushed to cope

with staggered starts, as in the Tour de France cycle race, or with thousands of runners pouring over the finishing line in the London or New York Marathons.

Chips to the rescue! Top-class races in everything from running to skating, cycling and motorsport, are timed by devices linked to the photo-finish mechanism, capable of giving times to the nearest 1/100 of a second. Staggered or mass start events, such as

a triathlon, are timed by attaching a chip to part of each competitor's clothing. For example, timing chips are often attached to competitors' shoe laces.

What the eye doesn't see, the touch pad will record. In the pool, times and positions are decided by the swimmer touching an electronic pad at the end of the race.

Timing swimmers Because water often obscures sight lines, swimming has developed a different technology. Sensors in the blocks record the start time. To complete a race and record a time, a finisher must touch a plastic pad. This instantly records the lane and the time, from which positions are clear. In 1987, on the first occasion this equipment was used, the competitors could not believe the times and turned violently on the judges. But a quick check showed that the equipment had worked perfectly.

TRIPPED CHIP

Finishing first in the 2006 Chicago Marathon, Kenyan runner Robert Cheruiyot tripped on a mat placed just before the finish, fell forward and knocked himself out. His body was over the line but his shoe laces with a timing chip embedded, were not. Result? The winner had not won – until his victory was confirmed by an old-fashioned stopwatch.

See it again The video replay is a key element of the modern sporting scene. It has a double function. The more forward-looking or go-ahead sports, such as rugby and cricket, use it as a way of checking decisions, while in others it is just part of the TV coverage. Replay evidence can also be used to root out foul play and cheating. Sometimes, a video screen can help competitors. Glancing up at the screen during the running race, for example, lets you see where the other runners are.

In sports where video replays are used, the pause, followed by the moment when an announcement such as 'Try/No Try' or 'Out/Not Out' flashes on a giant screen above the crowd, improves the match experience by adding an element of suspense. The decision is also correct, cutting out bitter post-match arguments. This is why video replay is permitted on a limited basis in several sports, including top-class American football, basketball and tennis. Some sports – most notably football and baseball – are reluctant to adopt decision-making technology. However, some controversial refereeing decisions at the 2010 football World Cup finals have reopened the debate in that sport.

Appeals Replay technology has introduced another, more controversial element to sport. This is the appeals system used in American football, basketball, tennis and, experimentally, in cricket. The idea is that a team (usually via the manager or coach) or an individual player is given a limited number of appeals against decisions that have not gone their way.

The best-known example is when a tennis player challenges a line judge's call. The appeal is referred to an official with access to technology. Although the decision is technically correct, the system introduces the tactic of appealing to destroy the concentration of an opponent.

American football's national league (NFL) allows limited appeals to a digital replay facility. Here a referee checks an incident on the video replay before making a decision.

FOR AND AGAINST

Does appealing to technology improve or spoil sport?

For
- Allowing players to appeal against decisions adds a new and exciting dimension to sports.
- Appeal to technology keeps human referees and umpires on their toes.
- The possibility of an appeal to technology makes it more likely that match-deciding decisions will be correct.

Against
- Appeals encourage bad sportsmanship as they can be used to unsettle an opponent.
- The authority of officials is undermined by an appeals system.
- Technological appeal is neither one thing nor another: if technology is always right, then use it all the time; if it is not, then don't use it at all.

Many argue that allowing tennis players to challenge the officials' calls, as Argentina's David Nalbandian is doing here, undermines their authority and brings the sport into disrepute.

Subtler and subtler Digital video evidence is old news. The latest decision-making machinery is based on military technology used in missile tracking systems. Hawk-Eye, the best-known version, is used in professional tennis. It employs a battery of at least six smart cameras to track and record the flight of a ball. Similar technology

HOW IT WORKS

Hawk-Eye works by feeding a number of consecutive images into a highly sophisticated computer programme that combines them into a single 3-D moving sequence. This is then relayed to a screen. The programme shows precisely what has happened – where a tennis ball has landed, for instance.

is used to record every movement made by a player during a match, allowing individual performances to be analysed in great detail.

We now have the digital technology to do everything an official does, and better – apart from punishing foul language and unsporting behaviour. Perhaps it won't be long before we have a robot capable of dealing with those issues, too.

The precise path of a tennis ball can be recreated on screen using digital cameras and computers. In the future tennis may allow all important decisions to be made, objectively, by machine. This could prevent arguments, and referees and line judges might no longer be needed.

WHAT'S NEXT?

On a baseball park or football pitch stand robots powered by solar panels. The decisions they give are correct every time and the players appreciate this. In 50 years' time robot umpires may well be the norm in first-class matches. Would we lose anything? Some believe we would lose the excitement of controversy, as well as the personal interaction between player and official.

ROLEX OFFICIAL REVIEW

CHAPTER 3
surfaces and stadiums

Stadiums like theatres, pitches like carpets, swimming pools like millponds, running tracks laid for record breaking ... technology gives the modern sport near-perfect conditions. Spectators, too, benefit from comfortable seats, TV screens and uninterrupted views of the action. Meanwhile, those at home can see the whole thing in high definition from their living rooms.

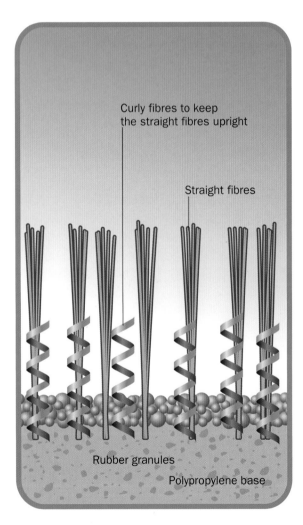

Many believe that it is only a matter of time before all professional sports, especially at the top level, are played on artificial surfaces like this.

Grass – real and plastic If there is one area in which technology has without doubt improved sport, it is playing surfaces. Today, we have pitches that remain green and firm all the year round.

Smooth playing surfaces are achieved either by having wholly artificial grass

HOW IT WORKS

Many modern sports pitches are a mixture of grass and plastic. This is so subtly done that the grass-plastic mix is invisible to the naked eye. To achieve this, the field of natural grass is sown by a computer-controlled machine that inserts millions of silicon-lubricated polypropylene blades among the roots of the natural grass. The result is the best of both worlds: the feel and cheapness of grass with the durability and drainage of a plastic pitch.

or by mixing grass with plastic fibres on a heated, well-drained, more traditional pitch. Where tall stadiums block out sunlight, ultra-violet lamps keep the grass green and healthy, and modern drainage systems mean that downpours no longer make surfaces unplayable.

Hard surfaces Two surfaces that owe everything to technology are found on synthetic running tracks and artificial tennis courts. Running surfaces vary from the older 'tartan' tracks of pure polyurethane to the latest mix of rubber granules in a polyurethane binder on a firm base. These tracks drain rapidly after rain. They are extremely expensive, however, widening the sporting gap between the rich nations and the rest.

WHAT'S NEXT?

Statistics show that footballers suffer fewer knee and ankle injuries while playing on artificial surfaces than on grass. As a result, it is likely that before long all top-class football, and probably most other sports too, will be played on artificial surfaces. An exception will always be five-day cricket, where pitch wear is an important part of the game. Spin bowlers, for instance, perform best on a worn pitch at the end of several days' cricket.

The surfaces of top synthetic athletics tracks are kinder on runners who trip and fall, reducing the risk of serious injury.

FOR AND AGAINST

In recent years all top-class field hockey has been played on plastic pitches regularly soaked in water ('water-based' pitches). This has caused much controversy.

For
- Hockey players say that a water-based pitch offers a more even and faster playing surface.
- Clubs and national associations have spent fortunes installing water-based pitches so they don't want to change them yet again.
- Top players have adjusted their game to the water-based pitch.

Against
- Water-based pitches are extremely expensive to install and maintain.
- Environmentalists say precious water should not be wasted on pitches.
- Countries like India and Pakistan, where water is not plentiful, are at a disadvantage if water-based pitches are the norm.

The modern range of high-tech tennis court surfaces makes the game more varied and more interesting. Alongside traditional grass, still used in Britain's Wimbledon tournament, there are 'hard', 'clay' and wooden courts. Hard courts have a concrete or asphalt base topped with acrylic or similar substance. Clay courts have little or no clay in them and have not done for many years. Instead, the base is topped with some sort of rubberised carpet layer. Wooden surfaces are most likely to be found at indoor courts where weatherproofing is not an issue.

Splash and dash Scientists involved in swimming pool design have come up with all kinds of devices to cut inter-lane disturbance. These include lane dividers and pool edges that absorb waves, and recycling pumps that maintain a smooth surface on the pool. All these improvements do not make much difference to the average person going to their local

ARTIFICIAL ATHLETE

The harder a running track, the faster athletes can go. To prevent things getting out of hand, a track's thickness and bounce is measured by an 'artificial athlete'. This is in fact a piece of machinery based around a metal tube with a spring inside. The running surface has to meet the standards set by the IAAF (International Association of Athletics Federations) in order for performances on it to be recognised.

HOW IT WORKS

Science dictates that to keep a pool as smooth as possible during a race it should be 2.2 metres (7.2 feet) deep so turbulence does not bounce back from the bottom. Sideways waves are cut by an extra, unused lane on either side and by perforated gutters that siphon off water and reintroduce it at the bottom of the pool. Bulkier lane dividers cut waves rather than ride over them.

swimming pool for a little exercise, but they make for fairer competition at the highest level.

Improved venues Back on dry land, venue technology spreads its benefits wider and wider. It brings glass squash courts that allow a much larger viewing area and better TV coverage, pitches made up of interlocking trays of turf that are easily replaced, snow machines to keep the skiers' piste usable, electronic ticketing in stadiums, super-absorbent safety cushions in jumping events … the list goes on and on.

This American football stadium in Arlington, Texas opened in 2009. It features a retractable roof and the largest high-definition video screen in the world.

CHAPTER 4
dressed for the part

Sportswear is now a billion dollar industry. Manufacturers make specific clothing for every sport and items such as rugby shirts have also become fashion garments. Moreover, some sports – such as top level windsurfing, skiing and American football – could not take place without modern protective clothing.

Wet and dry The ideal athletic garment should keep the wearer warm in the cold and cool in the heat. Research has come up with various solutions. 'Breathing' fabrics allow moisture (ie sweat) to pass from inside to out while not allowing rain to move the other way. 'Wicking' fabrics draw sweat away from the skin, allowing an athlete's body to save energy by keeping an even skin temperature.

Gases can travel through waterproof breathing fabrics but water is repelled.

HOW IT WORKS

Wicking fabrics work on the same principle as a candle wick. In a candle, the string, or wick, draws liquid fuel – usually melted candle wax – to the flame where it turns into vapour and burns. In a similar way, wicking fabrics draw moisture away from the surface of the skin and carry it to the outside of the material where it can evaporate freely. This allows the body's natural temperature control mechanism, which uses the evaporation of sweat to lower surface temperature, to work more efficiently. Moisture trapped next to the skin doesn't allow the cooling effect of evaporation to work.

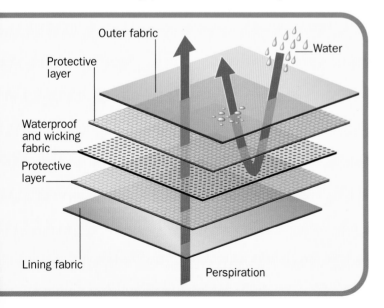

Outer fabric

Protective layer

Waterproof and wicking fabric

Protective layer

Water

Lining fabric

Perspiration

The very latest sports materials combine both water-attracting (hydrophilic) fibres to do the wicking and water-repelling (hydrophobic) fibres to do the breathing. On an even higher level are fabrics made with 'phase change' materials (PCMs). These are gels or waxes that absorb heat without gaining much heat themselves. Minute capsules of them are incorporated within the fabric of a sporting garment at the manufacturing stage, giving the wearer a much greater chance of staying cool in competition.

Full support It is almost impossible to imagine any sporting event without the synthetic fibre elastane. Because every thread is elastic, it combines support with flexibility. By holding muscles steady, it also helps blood flow and calms vibration.

A close-up picture of the surface of a 'shark-skin' swimsuit. The minute ridges mimic those on a shark's skin, reducing turbulence and therefore reducing drag through the water.

Similar claims are made for the shark-skin-type materials used for swimsuits. These are based on fish skin that has millions of minute, teeth-shaped scales all lying in the same direction.

FOR AND AGAINST

In recent years, hi-tech swimsuits have caused enormous controversy in pools around the world.

For
- Shark-skin and polyurethane swimsuits improve performance, allowing records to be broken. This increases the sport's popular appeal.
- The new swimsuits are more up-to-date, helping make the sport more attractive to TV audiences.
- A sport that turns its back on technological development presents an old-fashioned and out-of-date image.

Against
- Shark-skin-style swimsuits alter the characteristics of the human body, so changing the nature of the sport.
- High-tech swimsuits are very expensive, benefitting competitors from wealthy countries.
- If winning or losing is a matter of technology, fair play and good sportsmanship are undermined.

They create a minimum of turbulence when water passes across them in the same direction as they lie.

When it comes to toughness, modern synthetic fibres take all the beating they can get. Combinations of cotton, nylon, elastane and polyester are almost indestructible, so that ripped clothing – even in the toughest contact sports – is just about a thing of the past. There are football shirts designed to stretch huge distances when pulled, making it easier for referees to spot foul play. Even more revolutionary, 'sheer thickening' materials like d3o toughen up only when they are required to do so.

Sportswear is not just about looking good and maintaining an even temperature. Many activities – especially winter sports, the different

Sheer thickening materials consist of molecules that can change their properties in different situations.

HOW IT WORKS

If you stir honey, it becomes harder the quicker you move the spoon. Sheer thickening materials work in the same way: the greater the force exerted upon them, the harder they become. The change happens in 1/100th of a second. Padding is soft and pliable – until hit. Then it becomes rock solid. This is perfect for all contact sports like American football and rugby, and really useful for the helmets worn by cyclists and horse riders.

forms of motorised racing and American football – require strong physical protection. Formula 1 motor racing is the extreme example. A driver's many-layered overall suit enables him to survive temperatures

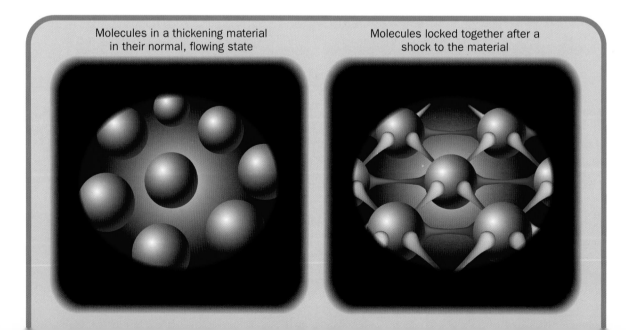

Molecules in a thickening material in their normal, flowing state

Molecules locked together after a shock to the material

of 850° C (1,560° F) for over half a minute yet still remain flexible enough to drive at 320 kph (200 mph)! The helmet that saved the life of Felipe Massa in a freak accident in 2009 was a lightweight, 17-layer minor miracle of fibre-reinforced resin over carbon fibre with added aramid (used in bulletproof vests), polyethylene, a flameproof layer and an epoxy resin binder incorporating aluminium and magnesium. Fully enclosed, it still permitted ten litres of fresh air to pass through it each second.

PERFORMANCE RATING

Sports scientists are working on trainers that contain movement sensors and an electronic chip. The chip is linked to a computer when the training session is finished and the athlete can read off detailed post-training printouts of their performance: how far they have travelled, how fast, stride pattern, etc. The information can be linked wirelessly to a computer and become to part of a comprehensive training programme.

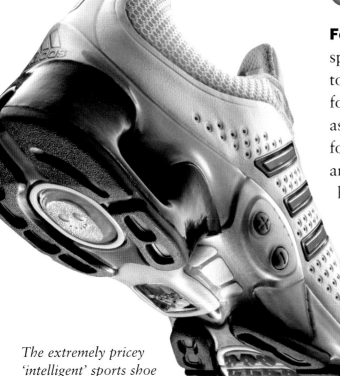

The extremely pricey 'intelligent' sports shoe has a built-in microchip that calculates the wearer's weight, pace and terrain and adjusts the cushioning accordingly.

Feet first The biggest impact of sports science on footwear has been to produce items designed specifically for each sport. So top-level footballers as well as rugby, Australian rules football, baseball, American football and field hockey players, all wear highly individual shoes.

Despite all the hours of research, there is still disagreement over what design works best. This is very noticeable with what goes on the bottom of football boots: studs or blades. Each has its supporters and researchers have yet to decide which gives the best possible combination of grip and quick release to avoid injury.

CHAPTER 5
sporting machinery

All sport involves technology at some level, even if it's just a starting line and a finishing post. But many of today's most exciting and popular sports – motor racing and skateboarding, for example – are actually created by technology. Technology has also given us new ways of playing old sports, such as roller hockey and water skiing, and the entirely new world of sport for those with disabilities.

New horizons Every weekend millions of people take part in sporting activities – on land or water, or even up in the air. Kids rumble around on skateboards, BMX riders hurl themselves round muddy tracks, and, on the lake, water skiers jump and dance behind powerboats. Up above, freefall parachutists float from a sky alive with hang gliders, paragliders and buzzing microlights. In short, technology + sport = something for everyone.

David Weir leading the London wheelchair marathon. No athletes have benefitted more from modern technology than those who were previously excluded by their disabilities.

WHAT'S NEXT?

Rowing boats with more than one body (known as a 'hull') would be more stable and therefore probably quicker. It would also be more efficient to have the pivots that hold the oars (riggers) moving backwards and forwards rather than the rower doing so on a sliding seat. Technology could bring both these improvements. It is only regulation that prevents change.

HOW IT WORKS

The paraglider is basically a huge fabric wing with a person suspended beneath. The wing is made of two layers of fabric joined to form cells, like a honeycomb. The front ('leading') edge of most cells is open, the rear closed. The wing holds its shape because air pushes into the cells and keeps them inflated, like a balloon.

Super machines – 4 wheels Sport technology reaches its pinnacle in motor racing's Formula 1 (F1). F1 cars may use only a 2.4 litre engine, the same size as a large family saloon. Amazingly, by reaching the maximum permitted 18,000 rpm (about three times the revs of a normal road car), the F1 racing machine achieves a stomach-churning 360 kph (220 mph) down the straight. On a tight bend the drivers' bodies may experience a force equivalent to over five times the force of gravity (5 g), close to the maximum a body can sustain.

In the interest of cost, safety and fairness, F1 strictly controls the materials used in the cars, their aerodynamic design and electronic input. This has been an area of much controversy over the years.

The joy of paragliding ... Technology does not just improve standards in traditional sports, it creates new ones and so widens popular choice and participation.

WHAT'S NEXT?

The noisy, polluting internal combustion engine is doomed. It won't be long before all cars are electric, and that will include the racing versions. But could you have a 320 kph (200 mph) battery-powered racer? It's certainly possible. The speed record for an electric vehicle is already around 350 kph (220 mph) over a short distance. Technology will soon enable such speeds to be maintained throughout an entire race.

One of the most interesting developments pioneered by F1 was the use of computers to get the maximum performance out of a car. Before the system was outlawed in 2007, computerised traction control worked out and applied the perfect grip of the tyres on the road and so replaced the driver as the judge of precisely how much power to apply at any given moment. This gave the best possible traction by eliminating inefficient wheel spin and the possibility of going out of control.

Technology is so essential to the success or otherwise of a grand prix car that critics say that car racing at this level is not really a sport at all.

Super machines – 2 wheels By comparison with F1, motorcycling and pedal cycling operate on comparatively small budgets. Nevertheless, the technology behind a 4-stroke 800 cc MotoGP (the motorcycle equivalent of F1) bike is right at the cutting edge, especially when it lets Dani Pedrosa's Repsol Honda RC212V power up to nearly 350 kph (220 mph).

To keep a machine on the track, tyre technology is as important as engine, aerodynamics and suspension. Both F1 and MotoGP allow a mix of soft (good grip but quick wearing) and hard (longer-lasting but less grip) tyres. The difference between four- and two-wheel adhesion is shown by the fact that a MotoGP bike circles the Spanish Jerez track in about 1 minute 40 seconds, while an F1 racer takes around 1 minute 17 seconds.

Obviously, you won't find those sort of speeds in cycle races. Nevertheless, the technological revolution has also worked its sporting magic in this field. The advances have been controversial, too, because teams that spend the most money can appear to get the best results. Track racers, road racers, mountain bikes, BMX … there's a machine for every cycle sport. Many bikes have frames of lightweight metals, such as titanium, carbon-fibre components and disc brakes.

HOW IT WORKS

Normal cycle brakes work by forcing hard rubber pads against the rim of the wheel. Friction causes the bike to slow. Disc brakes increase the amount of friction and are therefore more efficient, as well as less damaging to wheel rims. They operate with much larger pads gripping on either side of a large metal disc attached to the hub of the wheel. Because they are closer to the wheel hub they work better in wet weather, too.

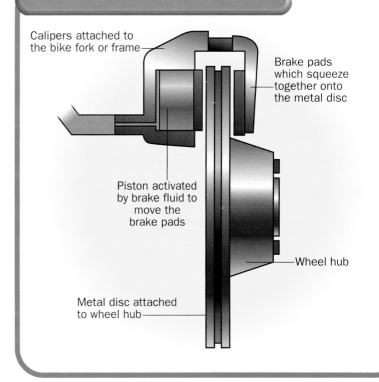

Calipers attached to the bike fork or frame

Brake pads which squeeze together onto the metal disc

Piston activated by brake fluid to move the brake pads

Wheel hub

Metal disc attached to wheel hub

Disc brakes increase the surface area of friction and so offer greater stopping power to any machine to which they are attached.

The modern track cycle is extremely high-tech – but still limited by the regulation that the rider must be above the machine and not in a more streamlined (and so far quicker) recumbent (lying-back) position.

The bicycle is the most efficient self-powered means of transport – but it could be improved. Engineers know that sitting on a bike causes more drag than lying back on it. Also, cyclists in a lying-back, or recumbent, position use their leg muscles more efficiently. The change to recumbent bicycles could happen if the cycle racing authorities gave it the green light.

FOR AND AGAINST

How much should cycling performance depend upon the technology of the machines and the rider's equipment?

For

- The technology that enabled Britain to win twice as many cycling medals as any other nation (14) in the 2008 Olympics has advanced the sport.
- Every country is free to develop similar technology.
- Cycling is a sport based on technology, so technical limits are artificial.

Against

- Britain's £26 million funding for cycling gave it an unfair advantage over other nations, especially developing countries.
- Sport is about human skill and determination, not who can build the best machine.
- Cycling events would be better if all competitors used identical machines.

Sport for all A modern wheelchair, with a frame of lightweight aluminium reinforced with tough titanium, now weighs around 8 kg (18 lb). A few years ago the equivalent machine weighed 23 kg (50 lb). Modern versions can be fitted with a fifth wheel for greater stability and the seat and rests are fully

SPRINGY LEGS

Aged 11 months, the South African athlete Oscar Pistorius (born 1986) had both his lower legs amputated. Technology came to his rescue when he was fitted with artificial lower limbs. These comprised two L-shaped carbon-fibre springs that were strapped on just below the knee. Controversially, they returned 80 per cent of the downward thrust of his legs, compared with about 45 per cent for an able-bodied athlete. Even so, he was still unable to beat top-class fully-limbed runners.

Scientists suggest that the artificial lower limbs worn by South African runner Oscar Pistorius give him greater spring off the track than an able-bodied athlete.

adjustable. These developments have opened up all kinds of opportunities for disabled athletes.

No longer confined to track and field events, the modern disabled athlete can take part in basketball, sporting dance, fencing, tennis and even football and rugby. For contact sports the chairs are fitted with guards and wheels that lean steeply inwards for extra stability.

Technology has also opened up the world of winter sports to disabled athletes, allowing them to zap down the slopes on specially constructed mono- or bi-skis. In the USA there is also the more dangerous fourcross machine, a sort of non-motorised go-cart in which disabled athletes career down mountains and leap ravines.

CHAPTER 6
training and cheating

Training for all serious sport is a tightly organised scientific process that cares for every aspect of an athlete's body and mind. At the top level the boundaries of what is and is not permitted are often blurred.

University level Around the world most self-respecting universities boast a sports science department. As a result, every avenue to sporting success has been analysed and plotted, and there are almost no top-class sportspeople whose lives are not arranged by others.

Motion capture: the athlete wears white reflective patches that enable his movements to be tracked accurately by video camera. Close analysis of the images will enable coaches to suggest how style and technique can be improved.

'Motion analysis' involves analysing a person's technique on computer via a digital camera. It is now basic to most training. Motion analysis is associated with more complex areas of study, like biomechanics, which is the study of the way forces act on or through the human body. Kinanthropometry, using data to predict a body's athletic potential, is another new area of research.

Another example of the influence of sports science is the fairly recent

HOW IT WORKS

Motion analysis takes many forms. At its simplest, it involves taking video of a sportsperson in action, perhaps from several angles, then replaying the movement in slow motion. This reveals weakness in technique that can be rectified. The athlete's performance may also be fed into a computer programme that compares it with a perfect model. This way, the athlete can see ways to improve their technique.

distinction between 'fast twitch' and ordinary muscles. Fast twitch muscles are essential for sprinting. In fact, it is now possible to analyse how much of each muscle type an athlete has and, before they run a race or even train, predict how well they will be able to perform.

Training Training is no longer about just 'getting fit'. Fitness is measured in precise detail. The most common device is the VO2 max test that measures the rate a body absorbs and uses oxygen.

Hopefuls who train and still perform poorly on the 'max test' might as well give up before they go any further: they were simply not born with a good enough heart-lung system.

A large part of athletic performance is linked to the body's ability to get oxygen from the lungs to the muscles as quickly and efficiently as possible. This task is performed by red blood cells. The body's production of red

HOW IT WORKS

The VO2 max test requires an athlete to take exercise that gradually becomes more strenuous. This is normally done on an exercise bike or a treadmill. The subject wears a mask with tubes attached through which all the air they inhale and exhale passes. The tubes are linked to machinery that measures the amount of oxygen and carbon dioxide present in air that is breathed in and out. VO2 max (level of fitness) is reached when the amount of oxygen the body uses remains the same even when the level of exercise increases.

The VO2 max test measures the efficiency of an athlete's heart-lung system. This reflects both the effectiveness of the system with which they were born (something that can't be changed) and their fitness (which can be improved).

blood cells is regulated by the hormone erythropoietin, better known as EPO. Basically, the more EPO in the body, the more red blood cells are produced and so the more oxygen gets to the muscles.

EPO can be taken – illegally – as a performance-enhancing substance or it can be increased naturally by living at altitude, ideally over 1,750 metres (5,740 feet) above sea level. Here the body senses the lack of oxygen in the air and produces more red blood cells. These remain in the system for a time after the athlete has returned to normal altitude. This is what is known as 'altitude training'. It can be mimicked by using an oxygen tent.

HOW IT WORKS

An oxygen tent should, in fact, be called a low-oxygen tent. It is air-tight and is filled with circulating air from which some of the oxygen has been removed. This mimics the condition at altitude where lowered oxygen levels cause the human body to produce more oxygen-carrying red blood cells. For a while these take more blood to the muscles – aiding recovery from injury – when normal conditions are restored.

Diet 'You are what you eat' the saying goes, and it is especially relevant to sportspeople. Food technologists have worked out that the ideal sporting diet is said to provide 60-70 per cent of calories from carbohydrates, 12 per cent from proteins and 18-28 per cent from fats. Before an event it is advisable to go in for 'carbohydrate loading'. This means stocking up on calories in the form of pasta or potatoes.

Most athletes eat bananas to give them extra energy. The way the body converts food into energy is now so well known that all top athletes follow carefully planned diets.

FOR AND AGAINST

The use of performance-enhancing drugs causes more argument than any other issue in sport.

For

- Some experts argue that all ways of improving performance should be allowed because they produce better and more exciting sport.
- As it is impossible to detect all drug abuse, it would be fairer to let athletes take what they want.

Against

- Taking substances that artificially improve performance is cheating.
- All sporting drugs carry serious health risks.
- If drugs were made legal, all sporting records would become meaningless.

Drugs There are more ways of cheating at sport than there are sports themselves. Many involve taking substances that are banned because they artificially improve the body's performance, giving an athlete an unfair advantage. All have seriously damaging side effects.

Testing for drugs is done by analysing samples of an athlete's urine and blood. The exact testing processes are secret, but we know blood testing, for example, involves separating blood cells from blood plasma by spinning in a centrifuge. In some countries this is done randomly all the year round; in others it is done

Sample testing for the 2010 Winter Olympics inside the anti-doping lab at the Olympic Oval, Richmond, Canada. Testers are always struggling to keep up with the secret laboratories that make a fortune from the manufacture of more and more sophisticated products to enhance performance.

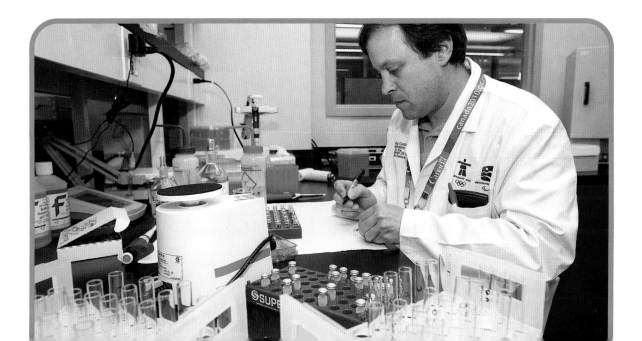

only in the competition season, enabling athletes to 'load up' on illegal substances in training but produce negative test results when competing.

The earliest performance-enhancing drugs included stimulants such as cocaine, as well as amphetamines that increase heart rate. Anabolic steroids that build muscle and power have been around for some time, too, but unscrupulous scientists are always producing new ones that are difficult to detect. The ever-growing list of banned steroids is now two pages long. It includes substances like zilpaterol, officially produced to fatten cattle, and nandrolone, which occurs naturally in the body in small quantities but which is regarded as illegal if more than 2 nanograms are found in every millilitre of urine. Since new steroids, legal and illegal, are produced every month or so, there is a continual game of cat and mouse between the drug-producers and the testing authorities trying to find ways of detecting the new substances.

Technology has also come up with various ways of cheating at drug tests. The cruder ones involve artificial body parts, such as hidden bladders filled with clean urine. Athletes can also take 'masking agents' that hide the presence of illegal drugs in their system.

More sophisticated methods of cheating include blood doping. This is

This banner is protesting against steroid use by US baseball players. Opinions about what athletes should and should not be allowed to take vary widely. Some argue that adults should be free to take anything they want – and accept the consequences if the long-term effects are harmful.

when an athlete's blood is taken from their body, concentrated to increase its red blood cell count, and then returned by transfusion to the body. A similar

WHAT'S NEXT?

Scientists are close to being able to grow human body parts from stem cells (cells capable of developing into all types of cell required in a living organism). From here the next step will be gene therapy. A footballer with a worn out knee or a javelin thrower with a badly damaged shoulder will be able to grow a replacement. Where will it end? Fifty-year-old discus throwers at the Olympics?

process is used with hormone doping. This involves giving athletes hormones, often harvested from dead bodies, that trigger things like growth or red blood cell production.

The ultimate technological cheat is to get the body to produce performance-improving substances on its own by genetic manipulation. If and when it does happen, testing for artificial performance enhancement will become virtually impossible.

HOW IT WORKS

Genetic manipulation or engineering in athletics means transplanting into the body a human gene (basic unit of heredity in a living organism) that produces a performance-enhancing protein or hormone. The process has worked with mice, enabling them to gain an extra 25 per cent of muscle in just three weeks. Officially, however, no one is quite sure whether it has yet been tried on people. Its consequences are potentially terrifying as it could cause changes to the personality as well as to the body.

Weight-lifting and body-building (shown here) are the two sports most frequently accused of using illegal muscle-building substances like steroids.

conclusion the sporting industry

Technology has benefitted sport in countless ways. It has raised performance, increased safety, created new sports and brought sport to those previously excluded. At the same time, it has turned sport into an industry, made top-level participation hideously expensive and, through the possibility of genetic doping, introduced a new world of cheating. Depending on one's point of view, the future is rosy – or dark.

Plus and minus The pleasure that a supreme footballer like Cristiano Ronaldo brings to millions worldwide is possible only through technology. His fitness, the carpet-like pitch, the state-of-the-art boots, the live TV images – all these things result from the application of science and technology

Equipment and clothing technologies have helped to raise standards and improve safety in winter sports such as skiing. Technology has also made it possible to create artificial snow at popular ski centres.

AN END TO RECORDS

The French Institute 'Irmes' reckons that top sportsmen and women perform at close to 99 per cent of the body's capacity. One hundred years ago this figure was 75 per cent. As the present rate of progress continues, we will get near 100 per cent by 2050. Ultimately, by around 2060, there will be no more world records – unless, of course, genetic engineering is allowed to produce 'super athletes' designed for optimum performance at a particular sport or event.

to sport. Such examples could be multiplied a thousand times over.

Add to this the explosion of disability sport and the host of new sports, from snowboarding to windsurfing, and the case in favour of technology seems unanswerable. But it is not.

In 2008, the top 20 of the Beijing Olympics medal table featured only two developing nations, Jamaica and Kenya. The message is clear: because the application of sporting technology – essential for success – is so expensive, medals go to the wealthy. Technology only emphasises the gap in the sporting world between the haves and the have-nots.

Sport is essentially about fun: exercise and competition for the sheer joy of it. Technology, in the form of broadcasting as well as equipment and facilities, has helped to undermine this attitude by turning sport into a business. Because so much money is involved, at the professional level winning has become its main purpose. Sadly, this attitude filters down to the school playground. Even here, gamesmanship can come before sportsmanship.

Finally, there is the grim grey shadow of doping. The list of those involved in doping scandals grows almost daily. And insiders say, we don't know half of what really goes on …

Track athletes from Africa dominate longer track and road races but lack of money means they cannot succeed in expensive hi-tech sports.

WHAT'S NEXT?

The market in steroids and other doping agents is worth several billion US dollars. The budget of the WADA (the World Anti-Doping Agency) is $25 million. Guess who wins? One answer could be to levy an anti-doping tax on all sporting transactions. This would give WADA the funds it needs to do its job adequately.

glossary

3-D Three-dimensional. Having length, width and depth.

acrylic A synthetic fibre.

aerodynamics The science of air flow around a physical object.

aramid An aromatic polyamide: a strong, heat-resistant synthetic fibre.

biomechanics The science of the forces acting on or through the human body.

boron An inactive element.

carbon fibre Graphite (carbon) in the form of fibre.

centrifuge A machine that rapidly spins a liquid in order to separate out its constituent ingredients.

ceramic An inorganic, non-metallic solid, often containing silicon.

composite Made of several materials.

curveball A swinging pitch in baseball.

d3o Lightweight and flexible materials that become hard on impact.

doping Taking substances that artificially enhance performance.

drag The resistance acting on a body as it passes through a liquid or gas.

drivers Golf clubs for long distance hitting; also known as 'woods'.

elastane a stretchy synthetic fibre used in clothing

EPO The hormone erythropoietin that stimulates red blood cell production.

epoxy resin A gluey mixture that contains oxygen, carbon and another element.

F1 Formula One, the premier motor racing organisation.

fibreglass A material made from fine fibres of glass mixed with a plastic.

free kick A football law that allows a team that has been fouled to take possession of the ball and kick it anywhere they want, even at the goal.

gene The complex chemical structure that is the basic building block of all forms of life.

graphite Carbon in its most stable form.

hormones The body's chemical messengers.

irons Angled golf clubs for hitting short distances with precision.

NFL The National Football League, the premier league of American football.

piezoelectric crystals Crystals that produce electricity when stressed.

piste An area of snow prepared for skiing.

pitcher A player who throws the ball in baseball.

polymer A large molecule with a structure in repeating units. DNA is the best-known natural polymer. Synthetic polymers are often plastics.

polypropylene A synthetic plastic polymer.

polyurethane A synthetic plastic polymer containing urethane.

silicon A non-metallic element that combines with oxygen and a metal to form one of many useful minerals.

steroids Drugs that mimic the male hormones and help build muscle.

synthetic Artificial.

tennis elbow Pain in the lower elbow usually caused by repetition of a vigorous action such as striking a tennis ball.

ultra-violet Light beyond the violet end of the spectrum, having radiation wavelengths less than that of visible light.

water-based pitch A hockey pitch with an artificial surface that needs to be heavily watered.

further information

Books

Higher, Further, Faster ... Is Technology Improving Sport? by Stewart Ross, Wiley, 2008.

Extreme Science: Secrets of Sport: The Technology That Makes Champions by James De Winter, A & C Black, 2008.

Websites

The official Formula 1 website:
http://www.formula1.com

A website with information about footballs:
http://www.soccerballworld.com/

These two websites look at sport and technology:
http://www.scenta.co.uk/sport/news.cfm
http://www.bbc.co.uk/worldservice/sci_tech/features/science_of_sport/

This website looks at the science of sport:
http://www.sportsscientists.com/

The Hawk-eye website:
http://www.hawkeyeinnovations.co.uk/Flasharea/Hawkeye.htm

This website has general news about a variety of sports:
http://news.bbc.co.uk/sport1/hi/academy/default.stm

A look at tennis technology:
http://www.tennisserver.com/set/set.html

Places to visit

You will find many of the technologies mentioned in this book, and perhaps people prepared to discuss them, at any sporting venue, including:

Your school or college sports department;

A local athletics track and field;

A major sports stadium;

A university sports department.

index

Numbers in *italic* refer to illustrations.